DRAW NEAR THE Cross

LENTEN DEVOTIONS FOR CHILDREN
AND THOSE WHO LOVE THEM

by Ellen Skatrud-Mickelson

AUGSBURG PUBLISHING HOUSE, MINNEAPOLIS

DRAW NEAR THE CROSS
Lenten Devotions for Children and Those Who Love Them

Copyright © 1985 Augsburg Publishing House

International Standard Book No. 0-8066-2200-8

Cover art by Koechel-Peterson Design

Illustrations by RKB Studios

The following hymn copyrights are acknowledged: "Deep Were His Wounds" copyright 1958 *Service Book and Hymnal;* "Lift High the Cross" copyright Hymns Ancient and Modern; "This Is the Spirit's Entry Now" copyright Thomas E. Herbranson; "Make Songs of Joy" copyright 1978 *Lutheran Book of Worship;* "The Royal Banners Forward Go" copyright The Church Pension Fund. Used by permission.

All rights reserved. Except for brief quotations in critical articles and reviews, no part of this book may be reproduced in any manner without prior written permission from the publisher. Write to: Permissions, Augsburg Publishing House, 426 South Fifth St., Box 1209, Minneapolis, MN 55440.

MANUFACTURED IN THE UNITED STATES OF AMERICA

Introduction

To Christians everywhere in the world the cross is a primary symbol of their faith. Its meaning derives from the manner in which Jesus died. He was crucified.

Death by crucifixion was a common means of execution in Roman days. It was intensely painful, humiliating, and cruel. Therefore it was reserved for those who were despised and who had no rank, status, or influence. To that kind of death Jesus Christ, the sinless Son of God, was subjected.

Because that death of Jesus, by God's wise and merciful purpose, made peace between us and God, Christians treasure the cross. It is a symbol of their salvation. The season of Lent, traditionally 40 days before Easter (not counting Sundays), each year renews and refreshes for us the significance of the cross. As we follow Jesus through the last painful days of his life before his crucifixion, the Holy Spirit moves us to respond in faith, hope, and love.

A symbol is never the reality. In using this book it will be important to explain that point. To wear a cross may testify that the wearer is a believer, but it can never guarantee it. The cross may be only an ornament.

Even the word, *symbol,* will need to be explained to children. A symbol is something to remind us of an event, a person, or some other reality. In this case we take the symbol to be something other than words. Candles on a birthday cake, for example, are symbols of years already lived. Statues and pictures are among the most easily interpreted symbols.

The book can help to give significance to the cross as a symbol of what Jesus means to Christians. But parents or other mature Christians will find it helpful to add their own comments to what is read and said. They should not hesitate to reflect aloud as the Scriptures are read or as the symbols are being considered. Questions, too, by parents to children and by children to parents are important to make these devotions live.

The charm and closeness of sharing one's Christian faith freely in a family setting through unhurried devotions will provide lifetime benefits. The elements suggested all have their value: Scripture readings, symbols, activities, and prayers. To make the most of this book all of them are to be combined in reverent and cheerful use.

First Week of Lent

The following mini-liturgy may be used each day in the first week of Lent. A cross, scripture lesson, activity, hymn stanza, and prayer are suggested for each day.

Mini-Liturgy

Leader: Let us pray. Thank you, God, for loving and forgiving us. Make your presence known to each of us. Teach us what Jesus' death on the cross means for us today. Amen

Scripture: *See suggestion for each day.*

Cross: *See suggestion for each day.*

Activity: *Prior to the devotional time, convert the cross or symbol for each day into a dot-to-dot drawing. Lay a piece of tissue paper over the drawing provided. Outline the figure with dots, numbering as you go. Some sections you may want or need to draw in. During the devotional time, children may connect the dots and color the cross or other symbol.*

Hymn: *See suggestion for each day.*

Prayer: *See suggestion for each day. Sentence prayers may be offered by each person by completing this sentence:* "Gracious God, as your forgiven people, help us to. . . ." *Follow with the Lord's Prayer.*

ASH WEDNESDAY

Scripture: John the Baptist preached that the kingdom of God was near. When Jesus came to him one day he announced that Jesus was the Lamb of God who would take away the sins of the world.

Read John 1:19-30.

Cross: The figure of a lamb holding a cross with a banner is called the *Agnus Dei,* which is Latin for "Lamb of God." The Agnus Dei symbolizes the wounded and crucified Christ whose blood was shed for us. The halo surrounding the lamb's head reminds us that Jesus is God's Son and, therefore, holy.

Hymn: "O Christ, Thou Lamb of God" (LBW #103*)

> O Christ, thou Lamb of God
> That takest away the sin of the world
> Have mercy upon us!
> O Christ, thou Lamb of God
> That takest away the sin of the world
> Have mercy upon us!
> O Christ, thou Lamb of God
> That takest away the sin of the world
> Grant us thy peace! Amen

---

*Hymn references are to *Lutheran Book of Worship*. The stanzas to the hymns may either be sung or read in unison.

Prayer: Dear Lord, you forgive us every day because of Jesus, help us to live each day for you. *(Add your own sentence prayers.)* Amen

THURSDAY

Scripture: Our sin separated us from God. But Jesus made peace between us by his death on the cross and brought God and people together again.

Read Colossians 1:19-20.

Cross: *The Iona Cross* is named after a large sixth-century cross that stands on the island of Iona in Scotland. The circle symbolizes eternity.

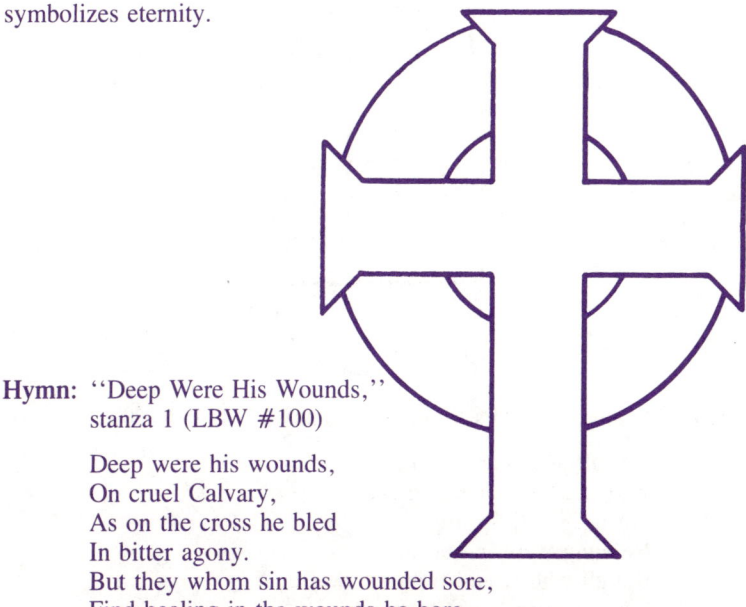

Hymn: "Deep Were His Wounds," stanza 1 (LBW #100)

> Deep were his wounds,
> On cruel Calvary,
> As on the cross he bled
> In bitter agony.
> But they whom sin has wounded sore,
> Find healing in the wounds he bore.

Prayer: Gracious God, as your forgiven people, help us to appreciate the great sacrifice Jesus made on the cross for us. *(Add your own sentence prayers.)* Amen

FRIDAY

Scripture: Jesus died but came back to life, never to die again. We, too, have victory over sin and death because we believe in Jesus.

Read Romans 6:9-11.

Cross: *The Cross of Triumph* has also been called *the Cross and the Orb*. The orb, or circle, represents the earth. The cross represents the triumph of Christ over the sin of the world. It also represents the spread of the gospel throughout the world.

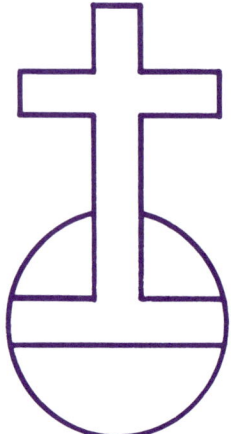

Hymn: "Deep Were His Wounds," stanza 2 (LBW #100)

> He suffered shame and scorn,
> And wretched dire disgrace;
> Forsaken and forlorn,
> He hung there in our place.
> But all who would from sin be free
> Look to his cross for victory.

Prayer: Dear Lord, you forgive us every day because of Jesus. Help us to celebrate your victory over the power of sin in our lives. Amen

SATURDAY

Scripture: We are invited to experience the great love of God, its "breadth and length and height and depth." This four-point description can suggest the picture of a cross in our minds.

Read Ephesians 3:17-19.

Cross: *The Cross Crosslet* is made up of four Latin crosses joined at their bases. It symbolizes the spread of Christianity to the east, to the west, to the north, and to the south.

Hymn: "Deep Were His Wounds," stanza 3 (LBW #100)

> His life, his all, he gave
> When he was crucified;
> Our burdened souls to save,
> What fearful death he died!
> But each of us, though dead in sin,
> Through him eternal life may win.

Prayer: Dear Lord, you forgive us every day because of Jesus. Help us to share the Christ who lives in our hearts with all the world. *(Add your own sentence prayers.)* Amen

Second Week of Lent

Mini-Liturgy

Leader: The cross of our Lord Jesus Christ appears in many places, proclaiming God's love for all people. Where have you seen it used? *(Take some time for discussion.)*

Scripture: *See suggestion for each day.*

Cross: *See suggestion for each day.*

Activity: *Make the cross or symbol for the day out of clay.*

Hymn: *See suggestion for each day.*

Prayer: *See suggestion for each day. Sentence prayers may be offered by each person by completing this sentence:* "Dear God, who gave us life, as people who have received the gift of your love, help us to. . . ." *Follow with the Lord's Prayer.*

SUNDAY

Scripture: Jesus was asked which commandment from God was the most important. Jesus gave a double answer: to love God and to love one another.

Read Matthew 22:37-40.

Cross: *The Latin Cross* is the most common form of the cross. This is probably the shape of the cross on which Jesus was crucified. This cross by itself reminds us of Jesus' being alive forevermore. As with all Christian crosses, the vertical bar symbolizes God's love for us and our love of God; while the horizontal bar symbolizes our love for each other.

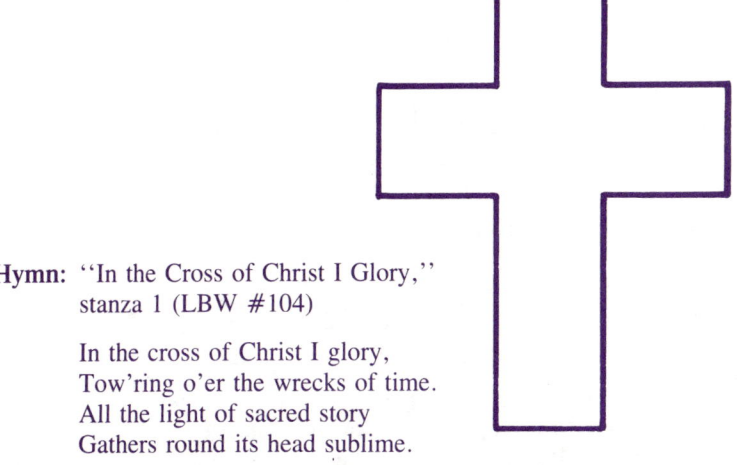

Hymn: "In the Cross of Christ I Glory," stanza 1 (LBW #104)

In the cross of Christ I glory,
Tow'ring o'er the wrecks of time.
All the light of sacred story
Gathers round its head sublime.

Prayer: Dear God, who gave us life, as people who have received the gift of your love, help us to love you and one another.
(Add your own sentence prayers.) Amen

MONDAY

Scripture: Jesus invites us to take up our cross and follow him.

Read Mark 8:34-35.

Cross: *The Greek Cross* has arms of equal length. It is the cross of mercy. For most people, they are first marked with the sign of the cross in their Baptism. The minister traces the sign of the cross (perhaps with oil) on the baptized person's forehead, saying, "Child of God, you have been sealed by the Holy Spirit and marked with the cross of Christ forever."

Many Christians make the sign of the cross while worshiping God. This is done by touching forehead, chest, left shoulder, then right shoulder with the thumb and first two fingers of the right hand. This reminds Christians that they are baptized in the name of the Triune God and that they are to take up their cross daily and follow Christ. *(Make the sign of the cross several times.)*

Hymn: "In the Cross of Christ I Glory," stanza 2 (LBW #104)

> When the woes of life o'ertake me
> Hopes deceive, and fears annoy,
> Never shall the cross forsake me;
> Lo, it glows with peace and joy.

Prayer: Dear God, who gave us life, as people who have received the gift of your love, help us to carry our crosses in this life. *(Add your own sentence prayers.)* Amen

TUESDAY

Scripture: Scripture teaches that because of Jesus' death on the cross we are reunited with God and welcomed into God's household, or family. All believers together make up the house of God, "a holy temple," as Ephesians calls it.

Read Ephesians 2:13-22.

Cross: *The Latin Cross Fimbriated* is a plain cross to which a fringe has been added.

Sometimes church buildings are built in the shape of a cross. The horizontal line of the cross divides the building into two sections. At the top of the cross is found the altar; the area below the altar is known as the *sanctuary* or the *chancel*. The area along the longer section of the vertical line of the cross and below the horizontal line is called the *nave,* where the worshipers sit. Some congregations have added seating with an extension of the horizontal line of the cross referred to as transepts. *(Discuss your church building and determine whether it is built in the shape of the cross.)*

Hymn: "In the Cross of Christ I Glory," stanza 3 (LBW #104)

> When the sun of bliss is beaming
> Light and love upon my way,
> From the cross the radiance streaming
> Adds more luster to the day.

Prayer: Dear God, who gave us life, as people who have received the gift of your love, help us to be a dwelling place for your Spirit. *(Add your own sentence prayers).* Amen

WEDNESDAY

Scripture: Three virtues describe the Christian's response to life. These are listed as faith, hope, and love.

Read 1 Corinthians 13:13.

Cross: *The Graded Cross* is also called *the Calvary Cross*. It is most often used as an altar cross. The three bars at the bottom represent steps or three different size squares upon which the cross sits. As the Calvary Cross these are symbolic of Mount Calvary where Jesus was crucified. In the Graded Cross the top step stands for *Faith,* which reminds us of our trust in the crucified Jesus. The middle step represents *Hope,* which points us to heaven. The bottom step represents *Love,* which describes God's actions toward us and our actions toward others.

Hymn: "In the Cross of Christ I Glory," stanza 4 (LBW #104)

> Bane and blessing, pain and pleasure,
> By the cross are sanctified;
> Peace is there that knows no measure,
> Joys that through all time abide.

Prayer: Dear God, who gave us life, as people who have received the gift of your love, help us to have faith, hope, and love. *(Add your own sentence prayers.)* Amen

THURSDAY

Scripture: Jesus promises us eternal life if we eat his flesh and drink his blood, which he gave up for us at Calvary. We understand this to mean believing in Jesus and having Holy Communion.

Read John 6:51-54.

Cross: *The Chi-Rho with the Alpha and Omega in a Circle.* The Chi-Rho is the oldest monogram referring to Christ. These are the first two letters in the Greek word for Christ. Both the circle and the alpha and omega, the first and last letters of the Greek alphabet, symbolize eternity. Together these symbols mean that Christ is without beginning or end. One place where this symbol is sometimes seen is on communion wafers. *(If your congregation uses communion wafers, check to see what symbols they have.)*

Hymn: "Jesus, Refuge of the Weary," stanza 1 (LBW #93)

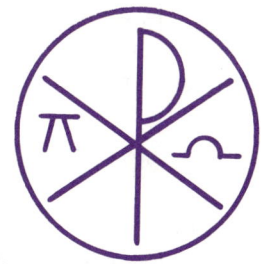

> Jesus, refuge of the weary,
> Blest redeemer, whom we love,
> Fountain in life's desert dreary,
> Savior from the world above:
> Often have your eyes, offended,
> Gazed upon the sinner's fall;
> Yet upon the cross extended,
> You have borne the pain of all.

Prayer: Dear God, who gave us life, as people who have received the gift of your love, help us to receive your gift of eternal life. *(Add your own sentence prayers.)* Amen

FRIDAY

Scripture: It is because of God's love for us, shown by sending his Son, Jesus, that we have eternal life.

Read John 3:16.

Cross: *The Celtic Cross* is named after people who lived a long time ago in the country we know as Ireland. The first Christian missionaries engraved this cross into stone slabs previously used for non-Christian worship. The circle with the cross symbolizes eternal life, in other words, the belief in life after death through Jesus' death and resurrection. The most common use of this cross is in cemeteries on headstones. *(Take the next opportunity you have to walk through a local cemetery to notice the crosses.)*

Hymn: "Jesus, Refuge of the Weary," stanza 2 (LBW #93)

> Do we pass the cross unheeding,
> Breathing no repentant vow,
> Though we see you wounded, bleeding,
> See your thorn-encircled brow?
> Yet your sinless death has brought us
> Life eternal, peace, and rest;
> Only what your grace has taught us
> Calms the sinner's deep distress.

Prayer: Dear God, who gave us life, as people who have received the gift of your love, help us to share the good news of your love for all people. *(Add your own sentence prayers.)* Amen

SATURDAY

Scripture: Some people think that Christ's death on the cross was foolish, but to Christians Christ's death on the cross reveals God's power.

Read 1 Corinthians 1:18.

Cross: *The Cross Aiguisee* is a variation of the Greek cross with a triangle at the end of each arm. The triangles point outward, reminding us that God's love in Jesus Christ is for all people. Another place where a cross can be seen for miles is on the church steeple. *(Take a drive the next opportunity you have and look for church steeples in your area.)*

Hymn: "Jesus, Refuge of the Weary," stanza 3 (LBW #93)

>Jesus, may our hearts be burning
>With more fervent love for you;
>May our eyes be ever turning
>To behold your cross anew;
>Till in glory, parted never
>From the blessed Savior's side,
>Graven in our hearts forever,
>Dwell the cross, the Crucified.

Prayer: Dear God who gave us life, as people who have received the gift of your love, help us to experience your power in the cross of Christ. *(Add your own sentence prayers.)* Amen

Third Week of Lent

Mini-Liturgy

Leader: Let us pray. Holy God, thank you for life and love and family. Please help us to know that you are always near. May the cross of Jesus remind us of your constant mercy. Amen

Cross: *See suggestion for each day.*

Scripture: *See suggestion for each day.*

Activity: *Make the cross suggested for the day out of pipe cleaners, using a styrofoam square for a base so the cross can stand up. On Thursday, instead of using pipe cleaners, color in a predrawn Luther's Seal.*

Hymn: *See suggestion for each day.*

Prayer: *See suggestion for each day. Sentence prayers may be offered by each person by completing this sentence:* "Dear Jesus, as we live under the sign of your cross, help us to. . . ." *Follow with the Lord's Prayer.*

SUNDAY

Scripture: During Jesus' life on earth he healed the sick and helped the needy, showing God's love for people.

Read Luke 6:17-19.

Cross: When the Greek Cross is colored red, it becomes the symbol of the worldwide health organization, the Red Cross. *The Red Cross* appears on ambulances, hospitals, and clinics, symbolizing care for the sick or injured. There are other crosses that are signs for providing care or mercy; these are called sanctuary crosses.

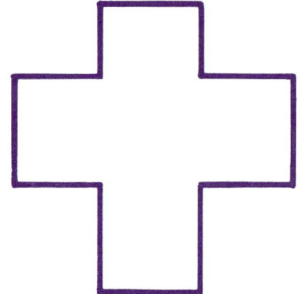

Hymn: "Lift High the Cross," stanza 1 (LBW #377)

> *(Refrain)* Lift high the cross, the love of Christ proclaim
> Till all the world adore his sacred name.
>
> Come, Christians, follow where our captain trod,
> Our king victorious, Christ, the Son of God. *(Repeat refrain)*

Prayer: Dear Jesus, as we live under the sign of your cross, help us to respond to the needs of others with compassion and mercy. *(Add your own sentence prayers.)* Amen

MONDAY

Scripture: Jesus taught his disciples that they could only grow and bear fruit spiritually by staying close to him.

Read John 15:1-11.

Cross: *The Budded Cross,* also called *the Cross Botonée,* is characterized by a cluster of three balls at the end of each arm. The cluster symbolizes the Trinity. The Budded Cross symbolizes the young Christian; whereas, the flowered cross, called *the Cross Fleurée* symbolizes the adult Christian. This form of the cross is often used as a processional cross. A processional cross is one attached to a long pole so it can be carried. *(Discuss whether or not your congregation has and uses a processional cross.)*

Hymn: "Lift High the Cross," stanza 2 (LBW #377)

> *(Refrain)* Lift high the cross, the love of Christ proclaim
> Till all the world adore his sacred name.
>
> Led on their way by his triumphant sign,
> The hosts of God in conqu'ring ranks combine.
> *(Repeat refrain)*

Prayer: Dear Jesus, as we live under the sign of your cross, help us to follow where you lead us. *(Add your own sentence prayers.)* Amen

TUESDAY

Scripture: We have hope in this life and for the life to come because Jesus has gone before us. The Scripture passage that follows may have inspired the Anchor Cross.

Read Hebrews 6:19-20.

Cross: *The Anchor Cross* is thought to be one of the earliest Christian symbols, along with the fish. The anchor was used as a way for Christians to identify other Christians during times of persecution, when they had to hold worship services in secret. It symbolizes the hope Christians have in Jesus' life, death, and resurrection.

Hymn: "Lift High the Cross," stanza 3 (LBW #377)

> *(Refrain)* Lift high the cross, the love of Christ proclaim
> Till all the world adore his sacred name.
>
> All newborn soldiers of the Crucified
> Bear on their brows the seal of him who died.
> *(Repeat refrain)*

Prayer: Dear Jesus, as we live under the sign of your cross, help us to have hope. *(Add your own sentence prayers.)* Amen

WEDNESDAY

Scripture: By wearing a cross as jewelry, we can be reminded that our bodies also belong to God.

Read Romans 12:1-2.

Cross: *The Adorned Cross* represents another use of the cross today, in jewelry, often in a necklace or pendant.

Hymn: "Lift High the Cross," stanza 4 (LBW #377)

(Refrain) Lift high the cross, the love of Christ proclaim
Till all the world adore his sacred name.

O Lord, once lifted on the glorious tree,
As thou hast promised, draw us all to thee.
(Repeat refrain)

Prayer: Dear Jesus, as we live under the sign of your cross, help us to take good care of our bodies and minds that we may have strength and skill to serve you. *(Add your own sentence prayers.)* Amen

THURSDAY

Scripture: The Bible has a lot to say about the heart. In our hearts we receive God's law. Since our sins are forgiven, we can worship God with a "pure heart."

Read Hebrews 10:12-25.

Cross: *Martin Luther's Seal,* also called *Martin Luther's Coat of Arms,* represents trust in God: "The Christian's heart is resting on roses E'en while beneath the cross it reposes." In the past, families and countries have used crosses in their coats of arms. They have even painted them on shields used in battle. These crosses are called heraldry crosses. Does your family have a coat of arms? Does it include a cross?

Hymn: "Lift High the Cross," stanza 5 (LBW #377)

> *(Refrain)* Lift high the cross, the love of Christ proclaim
> Till all the world adore his sacred name.
>
> So shall our song of triumph ever be:
> Praise to the Crucified for victory!
> *(Repeat refrain)*

Prayer: Dear Jesus, as we live under the sign of your cross, help us to worship you with a pure heart, in full assurance of faith. *(Add your own sentence prayers.)* Amen

FRIDAY

Scripture: Today's Scripture speaks of Andrew telling his brother, Peter, about the Messiah and bringing Peter to the Messiah, Jesus. Because of his act, Andrew has been called the first Christian missionary.

Read John 1:40-52.

Cross: *St. Andrew's Cross* resembles the letter X. According to tradition, the disciple Andrew was crucified in Greece on an X-shaped cross. The cross is often used in symbolizing individual martyrs and saints.

Hymn: "Take Up Your Cross, the Savior Said," stanza 1 (LBW #398)

"Take up your cross," the Savior said,
"If you would my disciple be;
Forsake the past, and come this day,
And humbly follow after me."

Prayer: Dear Jesus, as we live under the sign of your cross, help us to follow you even during the difficult times of life. *(Add your own sentence prayers.)* Amen

SATURDAY

Scripture: Read Paul's description of what life can be for those who follow Jesus.

Read Galatians 2:20.

Cross: *The Chi-Rho is a monogram. (See Thursday of the Second Week of Lent for the meaning.)* A monogram is a symbol made from some initials. Do you have a monogram for yourself?

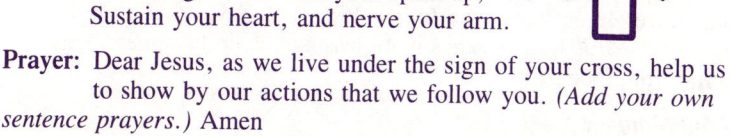

Hymn: "Take Up Your Cross, the Savior Said," stanza 2 (LBW #398)

Take up your cross; let not its weight
Pervade your soul with vain alarm;
His strength shall bear your spirit up,
Sustain your heart, and nerve your arm.

Prayer: Dear Jesus, as we live under the sign of your cross, help us to show by our actions that we follow you. *(Add your own sentence prayers.)* Amen

Fourth Week of Lent

Mini-Liturgy

Leader: Many forms of the cross of Jesus Christ have been made by artists through the centuries to proclaim God's love. What are some different crosses that we have already talked about?

Scripture: *See suggestion for each day.*

Cross: *See suggestion for each day.*

Activity: *On Sunday, Monday, and Saturday cut the crosses out of sponges, then use the sponges as stamps by dipping them in paint and setting them on paper. On the other days of this week, predraw the crosses and have the children color them.*

Hymn: *See suggestion for each day.*

Prayer: *Everyone join hands in a circle and pray in unison,* "God, keep us in the covenant of our Baptism. Amen." *Follow with the Lord's Prayer.*

SUNDAY

Scripture: Even those who follow Jesus will have troubles in life. But Jesus teaches that blessings, even happiness, can come from them.

Read Matthew 5:3-11.

Cross: *The Maltese Cross* is also called *the Cross of Regeneration.* The eight points at the ends of its arms represent the eight Beatitudes.

Hymn: "Love Consecrates the Humblest Act," stanza 1 (LBW #122)

> Love consecrates the humblest act
> And haloes mercy's deeds;
> It sheds a benediction sweet
> And hallows human needs.

MONDAY

Scripture: The "lifted up" in the scripture passage for today refers to Jesus' death on the cross.

Read John 3:14-15.

Cross: *The Tau Cross* takes its name from the Greek letter *T*. It is said to have been the shape of the staff Moses raised in the wilderness (Numbers 21:4-9). For this reason it is also called *the Cross of the Old Testament* or *the Prophetic Cross.*

Hymn: "Love Consecrates the Humblest Act," stanza 2 (LBW #122)

> When in the shadow of the cross
> Christ knelt and washed the feet
> Of his disciples, he gave us
> A sign of love complete.

TUESDAY

Scripture: The gospel of Jesus Christ has spread because the Holy Spirit gives people the power to witness.

Read Acts 1:8.

Cross: *The Jerusalem Cross,* also called *the Missionary Cross,* is made of four Tau crosses joined at their base and four Greek crosses. The five crosses remind us of the five wounds that Christ suffered while on the cross (hands, feet, and side). The Tau and Greek crosses can also symbolize that Jesus' death on the cross ended the Old Testament Law. As the Missionary Cross, the large central cross symbolizes Jerusalem and the four Greek crosses symbolize the four corners of the earth to which missionaries carry the message of Jesus Christ. This cross was first used during the Crusades, beginning in 1099 A.D.

Hymn: "Love Consecrates the Humblest Act," stanza 3 (LBW #122)

> Love serves and willing stoops to serve;
> What Christ in love so true
> Has freely done for one and all,
> Let us now gladly do!

WEDNESDAY

Scripture: The scripture passage for today is special in that it mentions all three persons of the Trinity, in whose name we baptize as Christians.

Read Matthew 28:19-20.

Cross: *The Cross Trefflée* resembles the Cross Botonée, except that it is fashioned after the Greek Cross rather than the Latin Cross. The trefoil at the end of each arm symbolizes the Trinity.

Hymn: "This Is the Spirit's Entry Now," stanza 1 (LBW #195)

> This is the Spirit's entry now:
> The water and the Word,
> The cross of Jesus on your brow,
> The seal both felt and heard.

THURSDAY

Scripture: In today's lesson, God promises us the crown of life.

Read Revelation 2:10.

Cross: *The Crown and Cross* symbol reminds those who believe in the death of Jesus Christ on the cross for them that they will receive the crown of life from God.

Hymn: "This Is the Spirit's Entry Now," stanza 2 (LBW #195)

> This miracle of life reborn
> Comes from the Lord of breath;
> The perfect man from life was torn;
> Our life comes from his death.

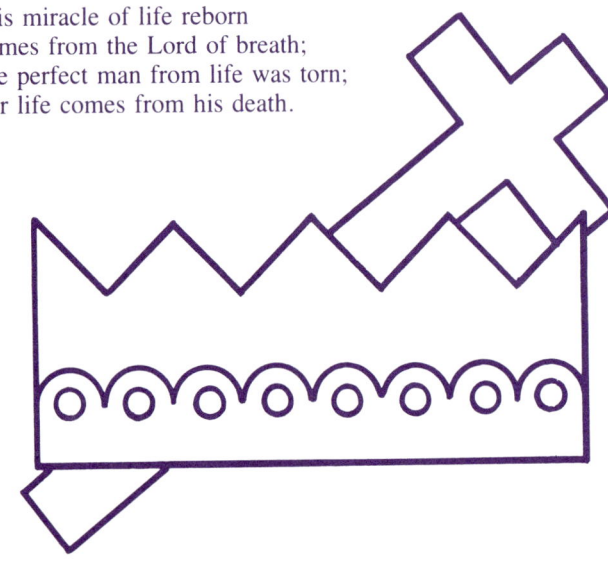

FRIDAY

Scripture: Today's scripture lesson indicates what part in the plan of salvation each person of the Trinity played. Listen for the mention of Father, Son, and Holy Spirit.

Read 1 John 5:5-9.

Cross: *The Cross and Triangle* combines the symbol of salvation and the symbol of the Trinity. It reminds us that salvation is the work of Jesus Christ, prompted by the love of the Father and received by people through the work of the Holy Spirit.

Hymn: "This Is the Spirit's Entry Now," stanza 3 (LBW #195)

> Let water be the sacred sign
> That we must die each day
> To rise again by his design
> As foll'wers of his way.

SATURDAY

Scripture: Peter's great confession of faith in Christ was followed by Jesus' prediction of his own death and the possible death of his followers.

Read Luke 9:18-24.

Cross: *Saint Peter's Cross,* as another martyr's cross, reminds us of the risk involved in serving Jesus Christ. Peter was put to death because of his faith in Jesus. He was crucified in Rome upside down because he felt unworthy to die the same way Jesus died.

Hymn: "This Is the Spirit's Entry Now," stanza 4 (LBW #195)

> Renewing Spirit, hear our praise
> For your baptismal pow'r
> That washes us through all our days.
> Lord, cleanse again this hour.

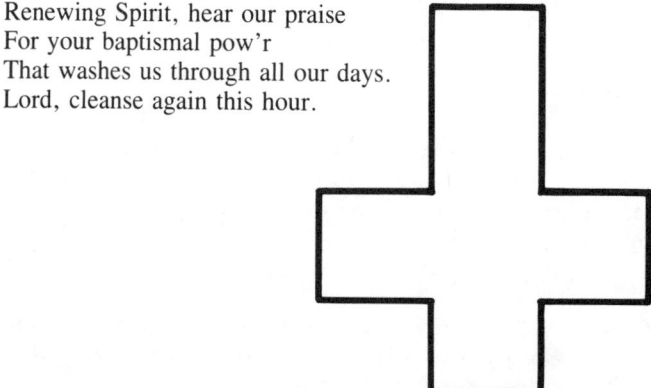

Fifth Week of Lent

Mini-Liturgy

Leader: Let us gather to worship in the name of the Triune God. Jesus promises us that where two or three come together in his name, he is there with them.

Cross: *See suggestion for each day.*

Scripture: *See suggestion for each day.*

Activity: *Glue felt onto predrawn crosses.*

Hymn: *See suggestion for each day.*

Prayer: *Each day pray for a different member of your family. This could include grandparents, aunts, uncles, or cousins.*
Follow with the Lord's Prayer.

SUNDAY

Scripture: Sundays are not included in the 40 days of Lent because all Sundays are feast days, celebrating the resurrection of Jesus Christ. Since Jesus has died and risen from the dead, we too shall live.

Read 1 Corinthians 15:20-23.

Cross: *The Easter Cross,* an empty cross decorated with lilies, reminds us of Jesus' resurrection. Lilies suggest the new life made possible by Jesus' resurrection.

Hymn: "Make Songs of Joy," stanzas 1 and 2 (LBW #150)

Make songs of joy to Christ, our head; Alleluia!
He lives again who once was dead! Alleluia!

Our life was purchased by his loss; Alleluia!
He died our death upon the cross. Alleluia!

MONDAY

Scripture: Today's lesson recounts Jesus' calling of the fishermen—Simon and Andrew, James and John—to be his disciples.

Read Mark 1:16-20.

Cross: *The Cross Barbée* is so called because the ends of the arms are barbed like fishhooks. This cross reminds us of our call to be fishers of men and women.

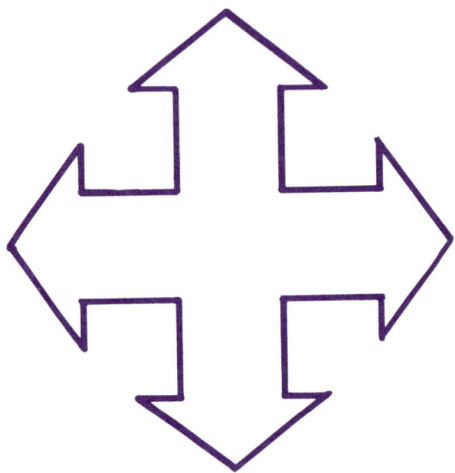

Hymn: "The Royal Banners Forward Go," stanza 1 (LBW #124)

> The royal banners forward go;
> The cross shines forth in mystic glow
> Where he, by whom our flesh was made,
> In that same flesh our ransom paid.

TUESDAY

Scripture: The gospel of John tells us that Jesus was put to death because he claimed to be a king. This threatened the Roman authorities. Jesus was crucified under the title "King of the Jews."

Read John 19:17-22.

Cross: *The Latin Cross with Scroll INRI* combines several symbols. The scroll represents the sign that Pilate hung on Jesus' cross. The initials *INRI* are from the Latin meaning, "Jesus of Nazareth, King of the Jews."

Hymn: "The Royal Banners Forward Go," stanza 2 (LBW #124)

> Where deep for us the spear was dyed,
> Life's torrent rushing from his side,
> To wash us in the precious flood
> Where flowed the water and the blood.

WEDNESDAY

Scripture: Before his death Jesus promised his disciples the gift of the Holy Spirit. We also have received this gift, along with the gift of peace.

Read John 14:25-27

Cross: *The Rainbow Cross* is a symbol of peace and reconciliation.

33

Hymn: "The Royal Banners Forward Go," stanza 3 (LBW #124)
(The word "tree" is another way of speaking of the cross of Jesus Christ.)

> Fulfilled is all that David told
> In true prophetic song of old,
> That God the nations' king should be
> And reign in triumph from the tree.

THURSDAY

Scripture: Jesus chose his disciples after spending an entire night in prayer. Today's lesson lists the names of the 12 apostles.

Read Luke 6:12-16.

Cross: *Christ and the 12 Apostles* are symbolized by intersecting crosses. The large, central Latin Cross represents Christ; the smaller crosses represent the 12 apostles.

Hymn: "The Royal Banners Forward Go," stanza 4 (LBW #124)

> O tree of beauty, tree most fair,
> Ordained those holy limbs to bear:
> Gone is your shame, each crimsoned bough
> Proclaims the King of glory now.

FRIDAY

Scripture: The throne of God is pictured with servants worshiping God who "shall rule for ever and ever."

Read Revelation 22:1-5.

Cross: *Christ Ruling the Universe* uses four crosses to indicate the four points of the compass and a circle to remind us that Christ is over all.

Hymn: "The Royal Banners Forward Go," stanza 5 (LBW #124)

> Blest tree, whose chosen branches bore
> The wealth that did the world restore,
> The price of humankind to pay,
> And spoil the spoiler of his prey.

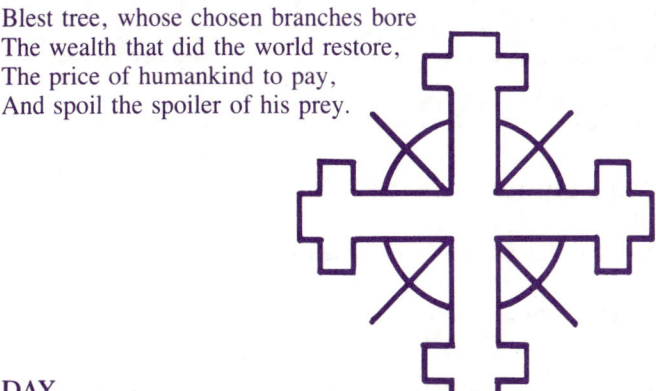

SATURDAY

Scripture: Although he was God, Jesus endured cruel mocking without complaining. This he did for our sake.

Read Mark 15:16-20.

Cross: *The Cross and Thorny Crown* reminds us of the crown of thorns placed on Jesus' head by the soldiers who made fun of him by dressing him up like a king.

Hymn: "The Royal Banners Forward Go," stanza 6 (LBW #124)

> To you, eternal Three in One,
> Our songs shall rise in unison;
> Those whom you ransom and restore
> Preserve and govern evermore.

Sixth Week of Lent

Mini-Liturgy

Leader: Let us pray. God of tenderness, hold our family in your loving arms as we live this day in your mercy. Help us to be loving to each other even as your love is shown to us in the cross of Jesus Christ. Amen

Cross: *See suggestion for each day.*

Scripture: *See suggestion for each day.*

Activity: *On the days Sunday through Friday make the crosses out of clay. On Saturday, if working with clay seems too difficult, have children color a predrawn cross.*

Hymn: *See suggestion for each day.*

Prayer: *Each day pray for a different neighbor or friend. Follow with the Lord's Prayer.*

SUNDAY

Scripture: The scripture reading for today includes a part of a prayer Jesus prayed just before his death. He prayed for us future believers that we might also share in his glory.

Read John 17:20-24.

Cross: *The Cross in Glory* is often used for Easter. A rising sun is positioned behind a Latin Cross so that the rays extend outward from the intersection of the arms.

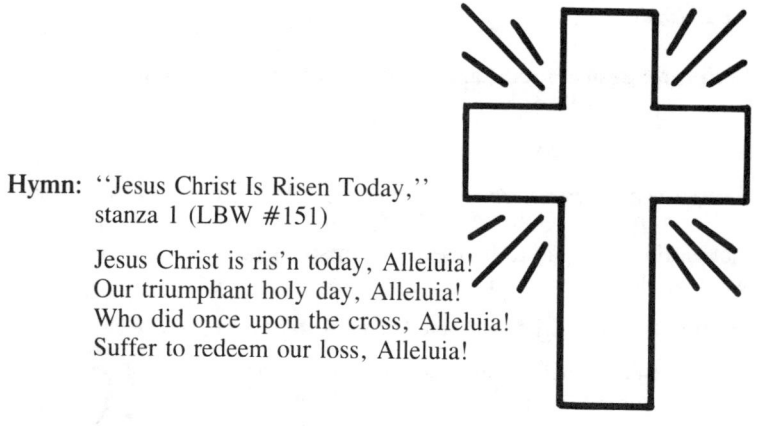

Hymn: "Jesus Christ Is Risen Today,"
stanza 1 (LBW #151)

> Jesus Christ is ris'n today, Alleluia!
> Our triumphant holy day, Alleluia!
> Who did once upon the cross, Alleluia!
> Suffer to redeem our loss, Alleluia!

MONDAY

Scripture: Jesus taught the disciples how to pray using the words that we know as the Lord's Prayer.

Read Luke 11:1-4.

Cross: *The Cross Fitchée* is any form of the cross whose bottom vertical arm is pointed. Used during the time of the Crusades, these crosses could easily be set into the ground when the Crusaders stopped on their journeys to pray.

Hymn: "Jesus Christ Is Risen Today," stanza 2 (LBW #151)

> Hymns of praise then let us sing, Alleluia!
> Unto Christ, our heav'nly king, Alleluia!
> Who endured the cross and grave, Alleluia!
> Sinners to redeem and save. Alleluia!

TUESDAY

Scripture: Jesus raised Lazarus and he will raise all the dead on the Last Day.

Read John 11:25-26.

Cross: *The Looped Cross,* also called *the Ansate Cross,* is an ancient Egyptian symbol for life. The oval at the top represents eternal life. It began to be used by Christians because through Jesus we have the gift of eternal life.

Hymn: "Jesus Christ Is Risen Today," stanza 3 (LBW #151)

> But the pains which he endured, Alleluia!
> Our salvation have procured, Alleluia!
> Now above the sky he's king, Alleluia!
> Where the angels ever sing. Alleluia!

WEDNESDAY

Scripture: Every Christian shows some fruit because of the Holy Spirit at work within.

Read Galatians 5:22-24.

Cross: *The Cross Pommée* is characterized by a circle on the end of its arms. The circles symbolize apples and, thus, the fruits of the Christian life.

Hymn: "Jesus Christ Is Risen Today," stanza 4 (LBW #151)

> Sing we to our God above, Alleluia!
> Praise eternal as his love, Alleluia!
> Praise him, all you heavenly host, Alleluia!
> Father, Son, and Holy Ghost. Alleluia!

THURSDAY

Scripture: Leaders in the church of Jesus Christ are to be a special kind of people. Today's Bible reading describes the qualities of a bishop.

Read Titus 1:7-9.

Cross: *The Patriarchal Cross* is usually worn by bishops. The shorter horizontal line represents the inscription, *"INRI,"* which was placed above the head of Jesus on the cross.

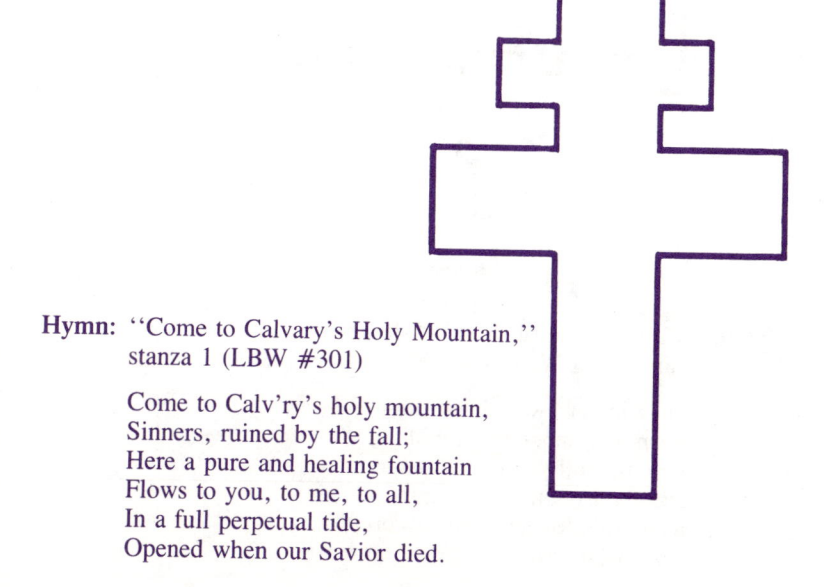

Hymn: "Come to Calvary's Holy Mountain," stanza 1 (LBW #301)

> Come to Calv'ry's holy mountain,
> Sinners, ruined by the fall;
> Here a pure and healing fountain
> Flows to you, to me, to all,
> In a full perpetual tide,
> Opened when our Savior died.

FRIDAY

Scripture: We are to follow Christ even if we suffer, because Jesus suffered on the cross for us.

Read 1 Peter 2:21-25.

Cross: *The Cross Crenellée* is an expanded form of the Cross Crosslet, representing the spread of Christianity in all four directions.

Hymn: "Come to Calvary's Holy Mountain," stanza 2 (LBW #301)

> Come in sorrow and contrition,
> Wounded, impotent, and blind;
> Here the guilty, free remission,
> Here the troubled peace my find.
> Health this fountain will restore;
> Those who drink shall thirst no more.

SATURDAY

Scripture: Today's scripture reading is the account of Jesus' entry into Jerusalem just before his death, when he is greeted as king.

Read Luke 19:29-38.

Cross: *The Christus Rex* translated means "Christ the King." This is another form of the crucifix, showing the body of Christ on the cross. The Christ figure wears a kingly crown and eucharistic vestments (dressed like a priest), representing Christ's rule over the world.

Hymn: "Come to Calvary's Holy Mountain," stanza 3 (LBW #301)

> Those who drink shall live forever;
> 'Tis a soul-renewing flood.
> God is faithful; God will never
> Break his covenant of blood,
> Signed when our redeemer died,
> Sealed when he was glorified.

Holy Week

Mini-Liturgy

Leader: Let us pray. O God of love and mercy, during this week we remember Jesus' last week before his death on the cross. Help us to realize what his death means for us. Amen

Scripture: *See suggestion for each day. The Bible readings are all from the gospel of Mark's account of Jesus' suffering and death.*

Cross: *See suggestion for each day.*

Activity: *All days except Tuesday, color predrawn crosses. After the crosses are colored, cut them up into pieces to make puzzles. On Tuesday make the cross out of clay and insert five red glass beads—four at the ends of the arms and the fifth in the middle.*

Hymn: *See suggestion for each day.*

Prayer: *Look through the newspaper or listen to the news to identify someone who might be suffering. Pray for that person. Follow with the Lord's Prayer.*

SUNDAY

Scripture: Today we will read about Jesus' entry into Jerusalem right before his death.

Read Mark 10:32-34 and Mark 11:1-10.

Cross: *The Cross and Orb with Palm Branches* combines several symbols. The palm branches symbolize victory. The circle symbolizes the world. The cross symbolizes Jesus' victory on the cross over the sin of the world.

Hymn: "Jesus, I Will Ponder Now," stanza 1 (LBW #115)

>Jesus, I will ponder now
>On your holy Passion;
>Let your Spirit now endow
>Me for meditation.
>Grant that I in love and faith
>May the image cherish
>Of your suff'ring, pain, and death,
>That I may not perish.

MONDAY

Scripture: During his final visit to Jerusalem, Jesus cleansed the temple and angered the religious leaders of that time, who looked for some way to get rid of Jesus.

Read Mark 11:15-26.

Cross: *The Cross of Golgotha* reminds us of the place where Jesus was crucified. The middle cross is for Christ; the other two crosses are for the criminals who died beside him.

Hymn: "Jesus, I Will Ponder Now," stanza 2 (LBW #115)

> Make me see your great distress,
> Anguish and affliction,
> Bonds and stripes and wretchedness
> And your crucifixion;
> Make me see how scourge and rod,
> Spear and nails, did wound you,
> How you died for those, O God,
> Who with thorns had crowned you.

TUESDAY

Scripture: In preparation for his own death, Jesus told a story about the tenants in a vineyard who killed the owner's son.

Read Mark 12:1-12.

Cross: *The Passion Cross* has many names: *Cross Undée* or *Cross Champion* or *Cross of Suffering*. The five circles represent the five wounds of Christ on his hands, his feet, and his side.

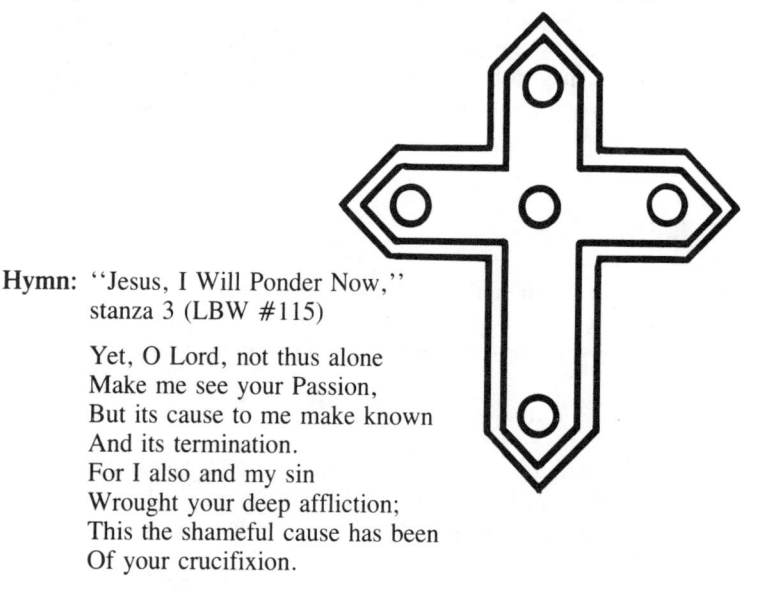

Hymn: "Jesus, I Will Ponder Now," stanza 3 (LBW #115)

> Yet, O Lord, not thus alone
> Make me see your Passion,
> But its cause to me make known
> And its termination.
> For I also and my sin
> Wrought your deep affliction;
> This the shameful cause has been
> Of your crucifixion.

WEDNESDAY

Scripture: In preparation for his death, Jesus is anointed by a woman with expensive perfumed oil.

Read Mark 14:1-9.

Cross: *The Cross Cantonée* consists of five Greek crosses. The five crosses symbolize the five wounds of Christ. This form of cross is often used on altar cloths and sacramental vessels or their coverings.

Hymn: "Jesus, I Will Ponder Now," stanza 4 (LBW #115)

> Let me view your pain and loss
> With repentant grieving,
> Nor prepare again your cross
> By unholy living.
> May I give you love for love!
> Hear me, O my Savior,
> That I may in heav'n above
> Sing your praise forever.

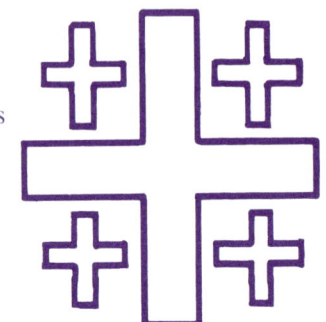

THURSDAY

Scripture: The Scriptures record the events that took place on Jesus' last night before his crucifixion the next day—supper with the 12 disciples, prayer in the garden of Gethsemane, and, finally, Jesus' arrest.

Read Mark 14:17-25; 32-46.

Cross: *The Passion Cross in Chalice* symbolizes Jesus' suffering at Gethsemane. In Matthew 26:39 Jesus prays, "My Father, if it be possible, let this cup pass from me; nevertheless, not as I will, but as thou wilt."

Hymn: "Beneath the Cross of Jesus," stanza 1 (LBW #107)

> Beneath the cross of Jesus
> I long to take my stand;
> The shadow of a mighty rock
> Within a weary land,
> A home within a wilderness,
> A rest upon the way,
> From the burning of the noontide heat
> And burdens of the day.

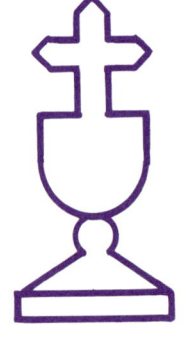

FRIDAY

Scripture: Today we read about the events of Jesus' last day—his trial before Pilate, his sentence of the death penalty, the soldiers making fun of him, the crucifixion, and his death.

Read Mark 15:1-41.

Cross: *The Crucifix* portrays the crucified Christ, reminding us of our Lord's suffering and the great sacrifice he made because of our sin.

Hymn: "Beneath the Cross of Jesus," stanza 2 (LBW #107)

> Upon the cross of Jesus
> My eye at times can see
> The very dying form of one
> Who suffered there for me.
> And from my contrite heart, with tears,
> Two wonders I confess:
> The wonder of his glorious love
> And my unworthiness.

SATURDAY

Scripture: After Jesus' death one man took courage and asked for Jesus' body that he might bury it properly.

Read Mark 15:42-47.

Cross: The message that Jesus Christ conquers is combined with a cross in this symbol. The top letters are abbreviations for "Jesus Christ;" the bottom letters mean "conquers" in the Greek language.

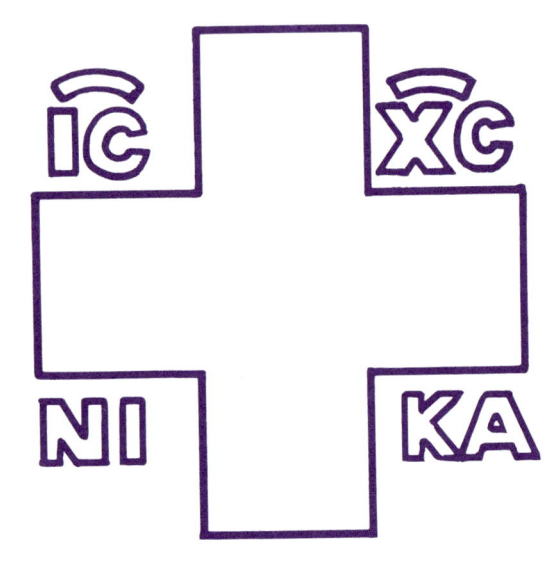

Hymn: "Beneath the Cross of Jesus," stanza 3 (LBW #107)

> I take, O cross, your shadow
> For my abiding place;
> I ask no other sunshine than
> The sunshine of his face;
> Content to let the world go by,
> To know no gain nor loss,
> My sinful self my only shame,
> My glory all, the cross.